I0796777

The Summer After

The Summer After

POEMS

Christopher Hewitt

WINNER OF THE NEW CRITERION POETRY PRIZE

First American edition published in 2025 by Criterion Books, an imprint of Encounter Books, an activity of Encounter for Culture and Education, Inc., a nonprofit, tax-exempt corporation.

www.newcriterion.com/poetryprize
www.encounterbooks.com

Manufactured in the United States and printed on acid-free paper. The paper used in this publication meets the minimum requirements of ANSI/NISO Z39.48–1992 (R 1997) (Permanence of Paper).

Library of Congress Cataloging-in-Publication Data

Names: Hewitt, Christopher, author.
Title: The summer after : poems / Christopher Hewitt.
Other titles: Summer after (Compilation)
Description: First American edition. | New York : Criterion Books, 2025.
Identifiers: LCCN 2024032760 (print) | LCCN 2024032761 (ebook) | ISBN 9781641774536 (board) | ISBN 9781641774543 (epub)
Subjects: LCGFT: Poetry.
Classification: LCC PS3608.E926 S86 2025 (print) | LCC PS3608.E926 (ebook) | DCC 811/.6–dc23/eng/20240719
LC record available at https://lccn.loc.gov/2024032760
LC ebook record available at https://lccn.loc.gov/2024032761

Contents

Acknowledgments

Grateful acknowledgment goes to the following publications in which these poems, some in earlier versions, first appeared:

32 Poems: "Reflections: Dallas" & "Wind on Market Street"
Able Muse: "Last Blue Hour at the Office"
Cathexis Poetry Northwest: "Lemons" & "Psyche in the Flying Glass Gazebo"
Ecotone: "After Reading about Decreasing Snowmelt in the Rocky Mountains"
Porter House Review: "Frost at Christ Church Meadow"
The Southampton Review: "The Glass Beach"
Tupelo Quarterly: "Cottonwood"

This manuscript was completed with the support of the Creative Writing Program at Cornell University and the Mario Einaudi Center for International Research, and much gratitude goes to these generous organizations.

Much gratitude goes also to Joanie Mackowski, Ishion Hutchinson, and Alice Fulton for their guidance; to Connie for pivotal inspiration; to Lucy Richards for her generous attention; to Maria-Ines and Wilson for the experiences that fed these poems; to Chester and Caitlin for help both on and off the page; to my parents for supporting my aspirations; and to Michael for all the rest.

For my parents,
for Lucy,
for Michael

The Summer After

Murano Figurines

We were fire and ooze, fluent in manganese
and other oxide salts reduced—or raised—
to the idiom of flux. We babbled, we bubbled.
What was the difference? What were differences?
Critically supple, spooled around an iron
spine, we were borne from our crucible
to a world whose surfaces—the marver, say—
bordered but never melded with the self.
Steel seared our yolk like snow. Our tissue hissed.
As starlings warble in one amoebic sweep
we twirled against the tug of the earth,
holding our scarlet congress, fumes of ire
aripple through the air. We were averse
to strictures of discipline yet too ungainly
not to submit. The blowtorch kept us raw.
Shears snipped us down to suns. A wooden slab
nudged us in shape. By then we joined the ruse,
persuaded by the eloquence of tongs
to sprout from silicate tendons wings or paws,
flippers or hooves, muzzles or manes, until
menageries with manners smooth enough
to decorate the shopfront shelf entice
the tourist's gaze with sparkling clarity.
Ecco! We harden toward our poise, our pose.
Rococo colors gleam like Italian ices.
Who shall adorn the zoo on your windowsill?
Swan, dolphin, lion, iguana, horse that rears,
a pale-blue snail, we brim with westward light and cast

luminous shadows, hectic script, our feral
treatise: if love is the way each stiff skin
loosens to merge with a liquid unity,
someday our benison may be to shatter.

After Reading about Decreasing Snowmelt in the Rocky Mountains

From the lecture-hall projector beams
a phantom glacier, filling the screen with a map of Colorado:
shadings from yellow to red convey declines in annual
snowfall. Orange saturates this ski town. Streams
narrow. A teenager flips through a manual,
cleaning her semiauto

for weekend mornings hunting elk
through Ponderosa pines each year less green, half of them tinder.
Down Main Street denim pockets jingle coins and keys
to pickups still uncaked with rocksalt. Skiers sulk.
An empty chairlift sways in a dry breeze.
The sun shines all winter.

Dishwashers languish, but the priest
tops off the holy water, hot springs steam, moon jellyfish
on the news swarm the vacant sea as chandeliers
the lighting aisle at Lowe's. Checkout lasers feast
on solar cell barcodes. Twilight spheres
the sky in nightmarish

translucence, adumbrates the day
the hydropower dries, though the neon vacancy at the motel
shines on, and preppers hoard bullets and batteries.
Monarch migrations dwindle, AM stations decay.
Thermometers fluctuate near thirty degrees.
A chickadee chimes like a bell.

The Glass Beach

No sooner do we see the sea glass shingle
than we fill our hands with brown globules,
blue oblongs, light-green jelly beans, labile
morsels on which the combers ruminate
so that these alcoves mash, hiss, and tinkle
like ice aswirl in a pitcher of lemonade—
precious garbage we too should leave alone
or worthless gems for anyone to own?

What we wish to preserve in a souvenir,
memory—made from what a Sumerian
called *baslu abnu*, molten stone—erodes
no less in the reef, or water doesn't ruin
so much as molt *le verre* we now revere.
As antiquarians savor every morpheme
scoring a cracked tablet, so one broods
on how a violet lozenge held perfume.

Minutes ooze, hands go numb, and fog
risen above the horizon wipes the slate
Pacific, blurring sea into cirrus. Vague
is every wave that scrolling inward rolls
across the brain. The mind, a rental tire
churning north—pulled by the Coriolis
force of community and the undertow
of desire—wanders off to contemplate

the asteroid belt. Four billion years ago
planetesimals filled the disc between Mars
and Jupiter; these larger bodies' orbital
energy sped them up so as not to accrue
but shatter on collision. Each asterisk
left after most of the particles blew away
footnotes an unborn Pluto, just as *why*
points back to some primordial arbiter.

Vamos a ver, a grandmother would say
on the existence of God or life after death,
rolling the R on her tongue, a hyaline
shard on a wave. Her decades as an alien
never polished her accent. *Wit* was "wheat."
Chuckling she'd mutter under her breath,
"life is a beach." Sea stacks stippled white
with seagulls hem this reef, so every day

through the first half of the twentieth century
as bulldozers shovel junk into the surf,
everyone's trust in the tide to flush debris
backfires. Backwashes. Breakers intumesce,
mull and mill the slowly shattering mass,
chime and sparkle with the waste of years,
recycle till they grind each edge to a curve.
Mini-moraine kaleidoscopes our shores.

Trash dump to tourist attraction: grace
or something like it—benevolent chaos?—
has made the backsliding rubble beautiful.
Pellucid tints of light, like tissues in fruit,

white window-moonstones fill the interval
we spend admiring what at a nearby kiosk
an artisan sands and sells, a newborn frit
entwined in silver wire. Worth its price?

Such gobbets less of reason than of rhyme
drew so many sifters like us that the town
outlawed glass collecting. From the crucible,
from the solar nebula, stardust in time
becoming this afterlife—look! A cerulean
dewdrop, halcyon pebble, glistening, wet,
cloudy when it dries, soft, porous, matte
as a grape with bloom, now irresistible.

Psyche in the Flying Glass Gazebo

Clouds swell and fall and roll
around these limpid columns; sofas for nymphs
and putti, cumuli-winnowings wreathe this craft in curls
of mist, condense to dew, and braille
the floor, beneath whose pane, as under ice, unfurls
a foothill. Day after day this avian glimpse:
the interstates unreel,

suburban streets expose
the whorl of a fingerprint. Whose light touch?
Farms patch a tablecloth where orchards of apple trees
foam up like whipped white canapés,
and a skyline crowns the plain with a Cubist congeries
of concrete. Canada geese, thank heavens, dodge
this airy cage or pause

on the handrail. They honk
and flap and lift and spell their southward V.
They dwindle toward the blinding haze where miles skew
the longitude. How strange to long
for air so thin, for earth so deep, for this cold bright sky.
Hail could crack the vessel, though the view,
so sweeping, so far flung,

sustains me. A hexagon
of triangles, the roof turns orange, pink
and cream, as do the clouds, until the total dark
when a winging shadow—pelican
or angel?—soars up here and lands. Mum as a shark,
he waits for me to sleep, or just to blink.
His nibbles dapple my skin.

Seafoam

Our café table bumps
a mural, a reef, its world a total façade.
A life-size lime-green moray eel
uncoils as if to flee the purple clumps
of coral flaking by our plates, while a cochineal
octopus oozes its arms to feel
the damages proceed.

Say that our palettes mix
acrylics instead of eggs and avocado,
that any world were ours to order—
would it order us? We sidestep broken tracts
down Judah. Crows convene on muni cables, quarter
notes on a staff, a Sunday murder
cawing its obbligato.

Wind weathers every dune
it sculpts. The surf, a downward pillowy
escalator, spills to the sand
which bent waves polish smooth all afternoon.
In glide enormous meringues of—ectoplasm? The strand
seems over-eager to daub the land
with spume. As buoys sway,

so the bubbles half reject,
half mingle with their moisture; lipids robe
in this structural ambivalence
an orb of air. Note how the skins reflect
cloud-filtered sealight through their layers, soapy tints
that marbling on the surface rinse
each miniscule globe

in Fauvist iridescence,
world aswirl in saffron, fuchsia, teal:
the marinade of animal grime
and petroleum distilled to sheer essence,
ichor whipped into bismuth-minted pearls that gleam
and burst before their milligram
mirrorings congeal.

Reflections: Dallas

On McKinney Avenue a mirror-sheen
of summer rain reconstitutes
myrtles in bloom. One pink blossom falls,
its holographic twin below the surface
rises, and they merge,

bridging the millimeter chasm where orange
cumulonimbi wander, miles
down in the shallows. Sidewalk paved with sky,
this heavenly mirage turns a newspaper sheet
to pulp and doppelgangs

towers at sunset, westward windows molten,
rippling when a rickety trolley
clangs to a stop, and a woman disembarks,
doused in a gown of diamonds. Meanwhile doves,
their feathers soft as receipts

tucked in a wallet, perch on a telephone wire
and ruffle from their wet gray wings
droplets that bubbling upward as they sink
riddle with brief concentric simmerings
the equivocal vitreous,

the asphalt's and the eye's—inverted images
counterbalancing concrete substance
with style. So that this walkway aquarelle,
distinctively selfless as the mockingbird's
recombinant pastiche,

flushed as with beta waves when evening lamps
rekindle their tungsten synapses
above, lays out an immaterial stage
for walking on clouds, a downward sky-high glimpse
reconceiving the real.

Notes on Aestheticism

A red-brick smokestack recollects
where a clifftop factory supplied
American shotguns. Now a phlox

of frost construes a sparkling glade,
though rockface icicles still pipette
droplets imbued with remnant lead.

Winter, spare industry whose peat
is absence, booms. Snowbanks control
the flume of footprints we impute

to cabin fever. The brookside trail
floods to a plane no bootheel cracks,
leaves stuck as in epoxy, mid-twirl.

Ice flounces like cooled candle wax,
carved to a winding concave sluice-
way purling with while it constricts

clear water—clear but with a glass-
green tint. Upstream, around a pool
revolves a slush of shattered floes.

The cataract looks blind and pale:
milk loaves on marble colonettes.
Whitewater plummetings compel

pinheads of mist to rise like gnats
and glaze an oak with layers of rime.
Fused to one side, the ice denotes

a second oak. White shadow. Limb,
branch, twig extruded into dream.

Juggling on a Nude Gay Beach

Blue, red, yellow, blue: three beanballs whirl
when a ripped trio—chiseled out by Blake?—
wades through undulant shatterings of beryl,

glistening head to glute. Collision! Fluke,
fiesta: two balls slap, the cascade explodes.
Balls everywhere. Some fellas "take a leak"

in the shady dunes. Not these three dudes.
On a blanket as on a Greek vase they spoon,
one in a jockstrap, one with nipple studs,

one inked on the arm: a howling blue baboon.
Pectorals? Plump as mangoes. Over them sways
an umbrella the hue of the lemon macaroon

one nibbles; over this a squawking freeze-
dry-weightless seagull spirals; higher still,
high, at least, as terrestrial wedding vows

travel, an octopus kite the thermals cajole
and blow to heaven tosses its radium-green
arms like a perm in a Mustang convertible.

Salud, dear juggling throuple. Dozens crane
their necks to watch. What joy in deviance.
May radiance bake our skin, sea salt prune

our fingertips, sea oats twine raw chintz.
A ball rolls off. The guy who grabs it grins.

Says the Water to the Wave

No sooner do you reach
me than my body gobbles up your soul,
for I am the medium your high-tide heavings roll
into this limber windrow, free
to roam the beach,

its green translucency
mounting potential as it swells and curves,
the flutes in the crest of its curl like stimulated nerves
aglitter, till the slope, too sheer
for symmetry,

spills, and headwinds clear
mist from the ridge, and we fold into our own
creation—you the subject, I the matter—and bemoan
our moment of hollowness before
the pipe you steer

explodes upon the shore.
Mingled with white noise we consummate
a slow disunion, fizzle over the shallows, our fate
to glaze the way for the next wave
and melt in its roar.

Sublunary Lovers

Like two hands grazing each other in the aluminum
hollow under a movie-ticket window, swapping
dog-eared bills for two seats in a luminous
dark, they no sooner touch than open
and pave subliminal

boulevards through each neurological metropolis.
They hang their fog machines in the amygdala
and on the hippocampus build their palace.
They take turns dragging as Magdalen
to watch Christ opalesce,

hovering from his tomb in Fra Angelico's fresco:
they kneel and lift their arms to clutch divinity
even as He says *Don't touch me*, an escrow
martyrdom empowering *Vinis*
vinifera to grow

fresh tendrils in May, though now in their infrared sauna,
robes on the floor, heat permeates each medium
down to the marrow. Gasps in a Vox Humana
warble out Te Deum per diem.
As the male piranha

hovers above his eggs for all three days they need to break
their pellicles and rise, the sinners grope Gamay
and after harvest—every cluster pregnant
with juice as radium with gamma
rays or a Scottish brogue

with rolling Rs—throw them in the barrel to decompose
in their own purple skins and three weeks later hatch
November's Beaujolais nouveau. When paws
grow cold, when owners' hands unlatch,
when Hallmark cards appease

the paper shredder's teeth, do cats gamble their final lives
to win nine more? What can we resurrect? Rewind
the tape, we'd say, as though to watch as loaves
unrise, or a rapid-healing wound
ejects its bullet. Christ leaves,

drifts over poppies red as the punctures through his feet
yet turns his head back to meet the gaze of the one
whose loss, come April when cardinals refute
the frost, mellows to joy. The sun
encompasses their fate.

Wind on Market Street

Where trolley wires seam the sky a crow
    parabolas and newsprint flits,
        folds, falls, and its spirit

moves closer—through the hair specifically,
    uncombing it as one ascends
        the muni escalator

and joins the impromptu choreography.
    A pearl-curtain of summer fog
        covers a hill where street-

lamps flicker, weak as tea lights; overhead
    the Castro's nylon rainbow flag
        large as a king-size sheet

lifts, and palm fronds mimic piano hands.
    Bougainvillea bracts on the sidewalk
        wobble through pirouettes

while cars stir up a crosswise current before
    the open door to the Midnight Sun
        where, on the lit stage,

a shimmying drag queen's vaporous purple wig
    billows above an electric fan
        and flings itself away.

Night Drive

After the loud crush, the club-light flux
refracted in ice and tiers of bottle glass—

now you're beside me in hermetic transit
back to your place, seatbelt cool, dash-

board digits rolling up a westward hill,
the rearview swallowing the city lights

while up ahead the sea-drawn fog dilutes
stoplights to auras, like overexposed film.

The halogen streetlamps' solitary pools
still cannot quite reconstitute the road

our driver's phone distills to backlit map;
we ghost by seaside townhouses, across

which ochre-lucid windows print already
forgotten interiors; the silver sheen of fan-

palm fronds dwindles forth in parallel rows
we hope to merge at last: your me, my you.

Nocturne

The moon adrift repaves the sea.
Suppose those opal cobblestones
bear weight. With equal buoyancy
we wander. Say the light sustains.

Who knows, we able simpletons
may find ourselves in a fluid loop.
We wonder. Say the light abstains.
How do we know until we leap?

My kind of salve, your fluent lip
undulates with the tide, my dear.
Wherever we go when we elope,
far be it from me to skip a dare.

Indolence whistles Fred Astaire,
so near and yet so far. Don't wake?
So be it. Romancing hips restore
the fraught tranquility of a wake.

Sonar and yachts and stars awake.
The moon adrift repaves the sea.
Freighters, quilting a gentle wake,
bear weight with equal buoyancy.

Frost at Christ Church Meadow

The cow pasture flooded and froze.
Over its milk-glass rink, two crows
    drift to a pine

and catch like bits of paper. Leaf-
less oak veins steam: auras lift
    an opaline

flue to the altostratus. Benches
stubbled with frost, icicle fringes
    still pristine,

here every footfall breaks a plate,
and scimitar edges tessellate
    the grass (still green).

Thumbprints thaw the windshield ice
whose crystal nexuses devise
    a dense star chart,

and the cow pasture, thinner at noon—
a glittering plane, scarcely known—
    breaks apart.

Lemons

If lead-paint chips poison the soil
in the backyard a smoke-blue ten-foot wall
encloses—patchwork plywood topped with curlicues
of razor wire—the lemon tree
still surges like some unmeltable fuse.

Branches, so densely knotted the leaves
stay stiff in a breeze, bloom and fruit all year.
Fleshy petals break on the thumb; each loose silk style
uplifts its stigma, the better to powder
with pollen. Too queer for the produce aisle,

turgid or tentacled windfalls bomb
the concrete, soften to mold or toughen to jerky,
save for the ones we tenants squeeze in the kitchen where
a rainbow magnet flags the fridge.
Lemons both endure and produce: they bear

the acid we mix with sugar and ice.
On a glass-top table the pitcher sweats citrines
that slide like us to the night when fairy lights entwine
the lemon crown with tinted bulbs.
The sinner builds a ruin, the queen a shrine,

and even after a thunderstorm
when a beam supporting half of the tree snaps,
sweeping the ground with flaccid wood, and when a leaf
turned over exposes citrus whiteflies,
lunar dandruff, the trunk falls not into grief

for severed limbs, but rather explodes
into green shoots, each lined with two-inch thorns.
One day within this fortress appears a hummingbird's nest—
a teacup woven from wisps of thistle,
floss, tinsel, and down plucked from her breast.

Flameworking

In a hissing torch's pale-blue stunbolt, glass
filaments drip off a red-tipped cane,
entangle, cool, in their crystal snarl weave
like evening swifts. The neural map a wave
lays shoreward. After class,

down la Fondamenta dei Vetrai, loose rain-
drops off an awning double beads
in shop-front necklaces, each globe a nonce
core of pure hue with copper continents
and their glittering terrain,

rose, white, honey, orange, blue, two breeds
of green—mint and the algae-rich
canal. A bare-skinned fisher's dinghy plows
a molten herringbone whose slosh-applause
slaps against and exceeds

the bank, sousing the walkway and the stitch
of a tablecloth. High noon alights.
Out from a trattoria's impervious glooms
a chef conveys a pizza topped with clams.
Its hot brine whiffs bewitch.

Two years of solitude. Connected flights
are wafting you around the earth.
Soon we may be a pair between whom sprouts
the bittersweet amber of an Aperol spritz,
awakening other delights,

a lamp left burning. Will satiation, mirth,
misgivings, reticence embark
on gondolas through tide-flushed arteries
that web these islands? Should we cauterize?
What is a history worth?

The teacher points to every fresh red mark
and faint white welt along his arms
and collar. Decades measured by the burn.
Even the morning when his kid was born
he rose to strike a spark

and twirl a lump and fabricate a farm's
worth of the pigs he had to sell
for baby formula. Forebears known as far
as the chronicles remember lived by fire
whose perduration harms

no more, his daughter says, than taking hell
from tourists, serving paradise
to tables round which no mouth even tries
to speak Italian, though it certainly chews.
Will we be that clientele?

Those nights your watch face whirled by the slice . . .
Each one the ash in the other's sand,
the blend unstable, quick to melt, each soma
flushed—should we reach that Serenissima
where glass recedes from ice

to fire, then let the next bead from my hand,
though wobbly, oval, crude, be yours.
Noonshards splintering off the ripples knit
on dockside hulls a luminous quivering net.
Then high tide floods the land.

Moonflake

Sand dollars map the daylight moon
along the tideline. Comber terraces
borrow their green from your irises.
Now I want the waves to be mine.

Along the surf, two pelicans soar,
dwindle beyond a beached red boat,
and near an airbrushed scarp afloat
on sea haze, fade in the dense air.

Today's last kite has already flown.
The sand crabs scuttle under rocks.
A moonflake in my pocket breaks,
exposing a foamy lattice of bone.

Another survives the walk home,
now worth its weight in the oxygen
we draw together, top with gin.
Morning heaps more ocean foam.

The Summer After

September. Ditch-side cattail fluff.
Disheveled gardens. Grill smoke. Plums
so ripe their skin, on the lip, splits.
The month hormonal pendulums
swing wide, off-kilter—golden tilts
the bat-entangled twilights slough.

The month when spider filaments,
linking your shower to the ceiling,
caught only the lightbulb's glow at four
in the morning, leftover Vaseline
rinsing below those seams on fire.
How easy the glide into romance!

Over the rain-dark sidewalk flock
another summer's maple boughs,
leaves curling while their edges rust;
the muggy noon, waxing bulbous,
darkens the watch tan off a wrist—
its vanishing too a kind of clock.

New alpha on Utica Street: a stag
in someone's garden, nipping kale,
raises his neck and swings his rack:
a threat or come-on, gall or guile,
tail flexed, fur rich as Armagnac—
what would you say, a total brag?

Those nights, how easily your skin
bruised, how untenable your veins,
your restless marrow minting blood
cells by the pint your doctor drains
each month. Prognosis: not good.
You told me this before we began,

and I—on my own and ravenous
for love, or its velvet shadow, lust—
thrilled to the speed of our covalent
bond which, too polarized to last,
tugged harder. Anxious to revel in
pulses our nerves alone finesse,

from duck-fat carnitas to cigarettes
to sunrise we sped to the afternoon
potluck where, after the fourth or so
Labatt, the hot tub foamed with none-
too-shy eruptions. Later you'd sigh
in the backseat. The end. Regrets?

None. Were we wrong to sanctify
indulgence—or wise to maximize
life by the hour? Here's gratitude
to you, dear end-of-summer muse
breathing *adieu*. Our web untied
its glisten. Now come days when I—

woah: as the sun leans, as the air
stiffens, out from behind me storms
a human blur, blue sweat-dyed shirt

unbuttoned, rippling back, his arms
laden with letters. Mailman Kurt.
Remember him? You liked his hair.

Sprinting across the lawn to clog
the slot in a door with envelopes,
he flaunts a messenger god's allure.
He pivots, gropes his duffle, leaps
where hot-pink chalk reads "Eleanor,"
repeats in cursive down the block.

From the Berkeley Hills

A sparrow, larger than the Golden Gate's
blue airbrushed silhouette across the water,
flits from a cypress, wilts to a millimeter
down where the traffic on Eighty granulates

to sugar crystals. Every BART train slides
eight matte-gray railcars, oblong beads on low-
gauge wire. Diminutive skyscrapers inlay
with glass the acres inching forth like tides.

Bungalows dwindle down this gentle slope
into redwood-nested geometrics, leaving
cirri to feather their vacuum. *C'est la vie*
said one who shared this view. A telescope

magnifies that tooth in the bay to a sail
unweaving the water's wrinkled gossamer—
or flipped around, concentrates the summer
cyan translucence all our lungs inhale.

The Dock

Careful. Ice enamels the planks. And strews a
cloud-white archipelago where the graphite
water courses north in a mile-wide furrow
plowed by an Ice Age

glacier. Finger Lakes they are called, these bodies
filled by streams that vein the terrain in central
New York State, arranged on a map like crooked
digits, no doubt, but

named because—according to legend hearsay
calls indigenous, though a Pilgrim might've
penned it—he who sculpted the world gouged them
out with his fingers.

From the bland white blindness of his perspective,
dustball-clustered snowflakes unloosen, slow as
floaters in the eye, and alight where mudflat
terraces measure

foot by foot the water's recession. Goose tracks
web the mire as highways the atlas, leading
nowhere, reconstruing their daydreams, always
changing direction.

Theirs is not the way of the runnels. Branches
wind, of course, but merge in a single lakeward
flume, engrave a print of the leafless pin oak
holding the shoreline.

Why? The shore has wandered a hundred meters
inward, where the Canada geese relocate,
blend their gaggles, float between floes, and nibble
something that ripples.

Cottonwood

Even if most of them never sprout,
these summer snowflakes, what a life, to skydive
from poplars, each tuft of down

both parachute and aureole, some
of them plunging, some drifting sideways, some
rising on mild drafts, and some

flirting with every direction, veering
and bobbing till indistinguishable from gnats.
Of course they all land somewhere,

on shadow-dappled ferns, the tennis
courts, the soccer field, the lake, transitioning
instantly from clouds to clods;

flotillas fuzz the brown-green water,
dip no more than a thread below the surface,
flouting the iceberg theory.

Is Hemingway wincing in his grave?
With a single green-flushed day to see the world,
who has time to be profound,

time for anything save relishing
appearances? Held to the eye, the fluff shrouds
the shoreside hills in cirrus,

as though the deity who chiseled
the land were a stuffed animal who flung his
innards across the sculpture,

quite literally expressing his own
inner life. Rubbed between finger and thumb,
the lint spins into a wisp

too glossy for cotton, more like silk,
with a limbo finish, not quite pearl or dust.
The seed is anonymous,

white, and flat as a dead fruit-fly
larva, but come evening, the airy fiber
fringes the asphalt walkway,

a surfline studied from an airplane
window, the rollers foaming onto black sand,
chewing away the continent.

Pahoa Bungalow

Drizzle simmers on the steel roof.
Daybreak slips through the mosquito net,
the cabin walls in the dawn light change,
now cyan, now seafoam, like shallows
seen from the airplane window, and over
these inner waters crawl a dozen gold dust
geckos from Madagascar. One green zig-
zag burrows behind a map on the wall:
wrinkled, soft, once folded in a pocket,
the island set with pushpins wears away
at the creases, where the paper frays,
as waves a few miles south break cliff-
sides down to columns. In the bathroom,
lava rocks worn to ovals, porous as sponges,
frame the mirror where another gecko,
skimming upon its own reflection, halts.
Orange Rorschach splotches on its back,
plump blue toes, limpid comma-claws:
the lizard licks an eyeball, bombs the sink
with a clump of undigested chitin, darts
to a wall-length window where not glass
but nylon mesh wards off the forest. Wild
pigs, a sow and her litter, black as the East
Shore beaches, barrel through underbrush;
alizarin feathers flicker up with a trill,
more flame and peal than bird in memory;
bamboo scissors, palm saws, bird-of-paradise
flowers that open like Swiss Army knives
dice the perspective into snippets of depth

where morning unfurls a million ferns,
shreds the clouds, and saturates the blue.
On the granite sink, a glint, a mica flake
—on closer scrutiny a bug wing, snipped
by gecko teeth perhaps—now blows away
like the blond hibiscus bush in bloom.

Scuba

One step for merman kind,
crash into molten tourmaline: cool
fizzlings creep through the neoprene suit, beguile
the skin to a bumpy rind.

Down in the foggy aqua
emerges an undulant mountain range
of coral, beige, green, pink, where sea whips fringe
boulders of curdled mocha.

Here lacy sea fans sway
like flattened oaks; here swells a brain
whose calcium grooves compose a maze prone
to fuddle the protégé.

Parrot fish, violet-teal,
crunch the coral. See one excrete
dissolving gossamer veils of fine white grout?
Sand is its finished meal.

It snows into crevices
where urchins—stars in negative—
needle their niches, where glassy fish eggs doff
their jelly, effervesce

into a massive school
of minnows: minor forms from Plato
minted, perhaps, from a sunken galleon's *plata*,
swishing fins of tulle,

snipped by a barracuda,
an eerily motionless two-foot spear
of black-barred platinum. Here predators pare
down bait like soft Gouda.

Here life doesn't buckle
no matter how many corals bleach
into marble tombstones of themselves, blotch
the technicolor, knuckle

the edge of a sudden cliff.
Where it drops into a darkening green
haze, while the lungs deflate, an unchecked groan
roils, and both legs go stiff.

Deep in that nothingness,
for reasons left undetermined, once
a divemaster sank, and sank, and did not wince
nor rise from the abyss.

Tempted? Who can say
or choose how deep the living go?
Still kicking, breathing, the body bubbles a roe
of spirit, up and away.

Time, too soon, to rise,
to watch the withering reef recede,
which may in part explain the divemaster's sad
yet ironbound demise,

for as the bionic self
ascends, the wish to linger weighs
it down, as if one could grow both old and wise
upon the coastal shelf,

letting barnacles cling
to the skull, octopus suckers drain
the heart, eels coil the hips, so that to drown
merely refills each lung.

Love's gravity increases
when love is a lobster, not a dove,
the salt in the blood a memory, and the dive
an undinal anamnesis.

Time at last to float
up and through the lilting silver
ceiling, the gauge needle licking its last sliver
just in sight of the boat.

Last Blue Hour at the Office

The monitor's liquid-crystal windows close,
and darkening blues—tinting the sky, the bay,
the watery clouds, the cloudy water—imbue
three years. Over a thousand afterglows.

As Whistler, for his nocturnes, layered coat
on coat of runny paint, so these spent days
accrue the mood of a falling gentian haze,
dilute the bayside skyline. Highways float.

Across the blue-green plate-glass highrises,
the crystal-liquid windows broadcast rooms,
fluorescent-white or lamplit-yellow dreams
made real. To whom? Directors, heiresses?

Diodes that pixelate the Bay Bridge swoops
and cables twinge like nerves in a waking limb,
glittering, while, from midnight blue to plum,
across the bay a heavier nightfall sweeps.

Vision at Dry Lagoon State Park

North on the road the redwood corridor
spills to a marsh across whose painterly
tuffets perspective, dilating, sweeps the shore,
the slate expanse, the vaporous horizon's
gradient blending the grays that underlie,
that overload a sky draped low with fog,
tulle that inland floats a mile and grazes
wooded hills whose glooms null an already
weak tin light—which like a mystagogue
discerns but a vague terrain yet intensifies
each green—here, turn down the radio,
stop. Let the wind, sheer fluency in search
of anything to break its passage, urge
on the ear its fast-and-loose philosophy.

Tousled as well by the gust, a shag rug
of sedge smothers the dunes, and off the trail
cruciform bootprints wander toward a rogue
relic by New World standards, sunk in sand—
Wayfarer Ray-Bans, black, always in style.
Be quick to lift them from the litterings
the tidal effusions issue, then rescind—
a beer can here, silvery driftwood there—
for a steel tsunami warning sign harangues
the drifter, preaching environmentalism:
NEVER TURN YOUR BACK ON THE OCEAN. To scare
recalcitrants, the pictogram's figure flees
a breaker's enormous claw. Planes, gulls, flies,
expansionists ignore the cataclysm.

Pacific? Currently more like Somnolent:
combers, no, rumples mustering the force
to rise shin-high, to curl partway, relent
at the surf, spill into bubbling varnish, nip
the toes, hold still for a half beat, reverse.
Giant mollusk withdrawing over and over,
mulling its calcium and quartz, the neap
tide chronically shrinks from any absolute,
invigorates the daydreamer's endeavor
to pinpoint frames of reference limber as this
eon-immune primordial surface dissolving
iron and bone. Why not these tinted lenses
salvaged from all the merchandise it cleanses,
wasting each mortar, each moral edifice?

From Gilgamesh who dreams of a meteor
to Gateway Tapes which lift the consciousness
out of the body, trances like mightier
radars expand terrestrial vision: grounds
on which the vagabond can roam and guess
how even the Great Pacific Garbage Patch
aswirl, by now the size of Greenland, grinds
down to a haven for jellyfish and snails,
how when the global heat hits fever pitch
and ocean currents cycle microscopic
plastics that foul the blood, the cardinal's
sermons, aflight from maple to maple, praise
the summer, though reefs bleach in a white daze.
Just now the water waxes hypnopompic:

that charcoal brushwork on the pewter sea,
at a closer look, becomes a seal. It lolls
on the ocean's tarnished mirror, courtesy
of the hologram the universe unfolds
and the slow spread of dominant alleles
through evolution and its harsh elisions.
Its fins don't care if they are energy fields,
nor do its whiskers twitch with sapience,
while here—beside the sedative oscillations,
rambling seaweed, tumble-polished pine—
these worn shades steep the sea in sepia.
The headwind formulates from saline fog
the crude morphology of wave-worn rock.
The rental Honda revs, and its wheels spin.

Song

Ramp up the lab or rub the lamp and ask the seersucker genie
to plop the moon in my hoola hoop, and Mars in your martini,
to pack each star in a music box that's neither timed nor tinny—
but will he scrap your reservations, make me feel less phony?

The cloud-bank rolls, the freesias blaze, the smoke alarm goes off.
Drunk angels throw confetti when you turn your head and cough.
Our neighbor says his man plays rough—but nails Rachmaninoff—
so his quiz gives birth to twins. Is love enough? Is love enough?

The beach umbrellas rebuff the sun with stripes of blue and white.
Sift through the photographs, my dear, and I'll go sift the wheat.
My mind becomes a clam and shuts, the better to gape and wait—
what for? What for indeed. A while, a watt. One smidge of wit.

Nothing is perfect, too—remember the swan in Amsterdam?
It swam all night in a trashed canal while the neon haze grew dim.
Sometimes the fountain opens a tab when you've only got a dime.
Here is the steeple, here are the people. Where is global doom?

Oh, slice a pear and dance, by George, whoever George may be!
May the grass be greenest where the power mower's on a spree.
The whiff of diesel's a doozy, but the tinsel of rain—well golly gee,
the roller coaster slides to its plunge, and we all go *we we we*.

Declivities

Down slopes that, spilling like rain-
streaks from the summit, web its face with snow,
past threadlike chairlift cables, the slow
weave of the eye-mote skiers carving up the fresh terrain,

the snowboard murmurs a sine
wave in powder. Side to side the U-chute curves.
Toe turn and heel turn. Gravity swerves
from edge to edge of the fiberglass. Snow lumps each pine

that rises ahead and then blurs
in the green stream peripheral vision slides
across on the way to mountainsides
as yet ungroomed. Slow down to finesse the conifers.

Pause for a breath in a copse.
A crow lifts off from a bough. Caw after caw
grows faint the farther it soars. In raw
silence made absolute by stillness, the crosswind stops.

Half to two-thirds of the trees:
needleless tinder. Snow doesn't cover them.
What pathogen is there to condemn?
Something digs even deeper than pleasure industries.

A ranger, at Boy Scout camp
one summer, peels the bark off a fallen bough,
revealing how through its sapwood plow
black beetles, carving sinuous grooves, the grain still damp

to the finger tracing turn
after turn their smooth, unkempt reticulum,
which fires reduce to a minimum.
Who would allow the forest, and our cabins, to burn?

Flight Patterns

Out from a stream-fed pine
the woodpecker skips on the air as a stone

on water. It lands on a trunk. Mist fumes
the gorge with the scent of wet

rust, and beyond the fly-fisher
whipping his filament over the surface,

across the steel bridge rattles a pickup
whose radio, casting its tinsel

out of a half-cranked window,
catches the ear—the twang of a banjo

nimble as burst fire bullets the factory
forged through the twentieth

century, its crumbling spillway
furry with mullein. The pileum feathers

raise a vermilion buzzsaw, the woodpecker
launches: wingbeats in frugal

salvos resemble the single
phone call a year sustaining our decade

of quips, the tinny thread of our small talk
unreeling its wavelength over

the country—double entendres,
punchlines, sinkers, hooks, tons of ammo.

The woodpecker rapping inscrutable Morse
on a telephone pole digs out

fresh craters—feasible grips
to climb for a glimpse across the valley?

Binoculars zoom to the hilltop cell site
spinning what lightspeed banter.

Annagrün

Uranus who first is the sky over Greece,
groom to the Earth, sire to Titans, evaporates
to ozone, the chaotic system of clouds,
much later in a backyard telescope reappears,
a pale-green marble adrift past Gemini,

no primal begetter, just some icy sphere,
both more and less material, sowing his marrow
in Saxon mines. Pitchblende, a mineral
bulbous and black as boiling tar, in nitric acid
and potash burns down to a yellow salt:

uranium oxide. Venting half-lives of ire,
this calx, mixed into glass, southeast in Bohemia,
colors a punch bowl the hue of Vaseline.
Annagelb it is called, after the maker's daughter.
Caught in tableware until the atom bomb,

it piques the twitter of a Geiger counter
and under a blacklight fulminates auroral green,
instilling in earrings, tea sets, candlesticks
the power that melts down to a magma whirligig
the core of the earth. Radioactive glass.

Add copper sulfate, and presto: *Annagrün*,
a green so searing that its emergence in the form
of a mold-blown candy jar, at a thrift store
in New York State, resembles not emerald, ocean,
grass, frog, apple, aphid, algae—but rather

the Texan sky when a supercell moves in.
Cumulonimbi tumble across the troposphere.
A distant thunder. Down Rosedale Avenue,
live oaks heave and azaleas soar in a green wind.
Tornado sirens whine. Again will twisters

tear the plate glass off a Dallas skyscraper?
Droplets freckle the sidewalk—a warning to hurry
indoors. A fusillade of phantom buckshot
slashes a window. Gray filaments, millions, plunge
in unison. Uranus, revived, has swooped

to earth. He rips off a limb from a backyard
peach tree; beyond it, a transformer clings to the top
of a power pole till lightning nails the box
and it explodes, deafening at least half of the block
and billowing perfect bright-blue rectangles.

Parthenogenesis

The Stoics believed the universe repeats,
so say we've slipped into these hotel sheets
    for the first time before and will again,
reliving the same lilacs, the same sleets—

do we affirm the frieze we'd cycle through
forever? Nietzsche implores us not to rue
    even the worst of our suffering, rather
to love it always. Swallow what you chew.

The future's behind us, and the past ahead.
We're Romans at a baseball game. Instead
    of nets and tridents, gloves and bats. Lions?
Mascots. Blood sublimates to infrared.

Amid an ephemeral cosmos which persists—
birthdays, fixed stars, Thanksgivings, taxes, cysts
    all swinging back around for another whirl—
the Red Wings play on like Neoplatonists,

their socks the same red as the clover mite
crawling across your knuckle: consummate
    vestal who never mates yet lays her eggs,
each one a clone. Imagine that. We might

transform into Athenas, float our genes
through eons as the Genesee River preens
    the selfsame frills, even though the water
braided into them slips and serpentines.

We'd pose on the Morgan Cup, a cameo
of white-on-cobalt glass whose homeo-
    stasis—less corporal than crystalline—
survives through Romulus and Romeo:

a maiden lifts a torch to a herm. His great
erection tapers—an oil funnel. Will fate
    grant her a child? Alas, she'll never know.
Her donkey only knows to stand and wait.

Behind, or ahead, tied to a tree branch, folds
of silk swoop over her bed. A satyr holds
    the other end, wraps it around a column,
flexing his goat tail, bane of prudes and scolds.

His legs, too long, too straight, betray a quirk
common in gems, not glass. The Roman work
    could be a copy! Still, to see it thrills
as when a batter hit the ball out of the park.

The Vampire Squid from Hell

Not a horror movie, this moniker, not
a vampire, nor squid, this cephalopod,
so what to call the lissome fossil
inhabiting the twilight zone where fish
wax eerie in the dark, compete

for garbage, deprived of warmth and oxygen?
Easing the high pressure with its facile
buoyancy, the gelatin blimp soars
into the floodlight—halt the submarine!
To eke splendor from refusal

dazzles the libertine. Its orange-crimson
head unfurls a pair of elephant ears
for fins; the languorous tentacles,
webbed like bat wings, ripple a taffeta
parasol, opalesce. Who dares

to roam "the land of both shadow and substance"
risks, on a red-eye, throwing integrals
out the window where, in the slashing
rain, a gremlin—bigfoot or teddy bear—
walks up the wing and ridicules

with its rubber frown the left brain's calculus.
Feral reflection. Fear? Awe. Malicious
enigmas bubbling up from Jung's
abyss—Dracula, Cthulhu, Lucifer—
spurred by a cryptic volition

share their ingredients with deep-sea fauna.
Nightmares are true. Imagination yangs
reality's yin. How else to pierce
the shadow but with lights we fabulate
from our nocturnal dallyings

with monsters? Likewise the coleoid contains,
in its false eyes and tentacle tips, spores
which glow by burning luciferin.
When under threat it spews glittering ink
and in the dazzle disappears.

Midnight Finale

Webs, interwoven, gauze
the streetlamp's octagon
of yellow panes. A key's

zigzagging teeth depict
the flit of mayflies lured
to the diode. Final Act.

Whom do you wish, Milord,
cult worshippers inquire,
skin slippery with lard,

ringing around the fire
in a TV drama. *Just one?*
Frenetic wingings veer

too late, crash into wan
voile, and the tense net
quivers. It's Halloween

all summer. Silhouette
crisp on a backlit pane,
forelimbs to spinneret,

funambulist on pinpoint
stilts: the weaver down
a guyline mimes Chopin

arpeggios for the dinner
guest it poisons, dresses
in silk. The organ donor

ripens and deliquesces;
the nutritive sacrifice,
irked by second guesses,

twitches, raising a fuss
across the network, bug
in the software edifice

the nimbly jointed legs
reknit, each neural link
receptive to what clogs

or snaps or twists a kink
within its consciousness.
How physical. To think

means simply to finesse
the high-wire gossamer.
The mind is ravenous.

Nightly a new premiere?
The deity wants more.

Phoenix dactylifera

Its argyle trunk goes up in fronds. A summer
tanager, up from the palm into Key West blush
aflicker, melts. Glints in a cloudbank simmer,

brighten, swell, and angling down in a rush
turn into jets when they hit the tarmac. Ropy
mangroves weave a revitalized underbrush.

To this balcony sea breeze wafts what therapy.
Stooges for over—twelve years now, thirteen?—
we still keep pace with our weltering entropy.

Swapping and scooping a spoon into a green
guanabana's milky-velvet mousse, each friend
plucks fruit from the sunset: guava, tangerine.

The blaze, in hindsight, foretells another end,
next year, at the columbarium, where noon
withdraws what shadows otherwise subtend

the buttonwoods, and where in the saturnine
shade of its niche now rests a blue bronze urn.
Your father's. More than ever now unknown,

he's left an ounce of ash—or so we discern.
Phoenicians pulped a thousand murex glands
for a pinch of Tyrian purple. What must burn

to pigment: does it brighten with each cleanse
and prove so strong that a couple droplets dye
the twilight? On Roosevelt Boulevard the lanes

curve where the night unites the sea and sky.
Swells crash. Stars immolate themselves to shine.
Our bicycles clatter. Scattered porch lights fly.

Duval Street. Apparitional throngs of wine-
and-diners, families, drag queens, bachelorettes
suggest that the afterlife—by whose design?—

conscripts the demographic range, the rights,
the spoils, and the thirst of a late democracy.
No one we know. One threadbare soul berates

the moon. Could he be—no, too dark to see
his features, whether they resemble yours,
and the rum blurs the hour, and the fallacy

of recreation (that travel smooths out years
from the face, the sunkissed keratosis) fades
to a dream of ancient Tyre: no one demurs,

behind a bronze mask, when the fire invades
the wood and oil we stand on, eager to bloom
for Melqart so he'll crush the Roman raids.

Sunrise. A child at thirty weeks in the womb
can see a flashlight held to the skin, the veins,
the membrane close around it, crimson room

aflush, and we too wake when sunlight fans
into these key-lime walls, this rumpled sheet.
The beach sparkles with molten dorsal fins.

At the cemetery we note which names repeat.
White sepulchres stacked like cargo on a barge
hold ancestors neither sleepless in the heat

nor dreaming next to offspring now in charge,
bless them, to whom the air is a steamed sauna.
The destination must be astoundingly large.

When we leave, let us recall how once upon a
tomb on this island, white slab cracked, we spied
no skull, no spine—but a lettuce-green iguana.

The hatchling, clawing away with the speed
of a dactyl, a trio of syllables, one for each bone
in a finger, thrived without a bible or spade.

Dear friend, may another decade, boom or bane,
dispatch to our plebeian skies a gold tribune.

Afflatus

I'd be the blue-green sweat bee lapping salt
exalted through your shirt—the best result
of jogging. Woozy off your glistening silt,

I'd slumber on your collar. Poplars swell,
lungs fill along this trail, the wind's a swill
of self these mid-May afternoons exhale,

and dandelion blowballs rise like bubbles
in sparkling water, popping their palpable
signals. Far on the lake a sunfish bobbles.

They all agree, the streamlines I consult,
that I should be the sweat bee lapping salt
while purple-martin piccolo notes exult.

Jogging in Spring

White petals steeped in watermelon pink,
the magnolia's origami
snowfall polka-dots the millipede

reel of the sidewalk. Femoral ligaments
tether swinging femurs
to pelvic wings: what a rigmarole

to nurture gumption. Negative lymphoma
tests impel a guardian
angel to pose a Greek amphora's

nude as inspo, loosen the cochlea's Gordian
nautilus, ease the crease
in the brow, prescribe more cardio.

The evening hovers at seventy degrees.
Lake Merritt's waterside
lampposts mottled with verdigris,

the promenade twisting as if to intercede
for kismet: are the nouns
in the shore's anatomy better said

while breathless? Docks to the left peninsula
water the tint of strong
black tea. Briny whiffs announce

the bay. Folks to the right laze in triangles,
trapezoids, ovals, rows,
dilating forth from homunculi

to grill-and-cooler enclaves miming Seurat's
A Sunday on La Grande
Jatte, while a rottweiler disarrays

a flock of gulls; from a lawn lucid-green
as chrysolite they rise
in hominy spirals. Ludicrous

as highway interchanges, let the arteries
hurl their forked ends
against a headwind, corduroy's

laminar streamlines. Let the sunset's bronze-
to-violet ombré sift
between jittery fan-palm fronds

while stars resist the increasingly abrasive
nightfall, every node
in the body's pointillism praising

the run-on sentence of the winding road.

The Quartz Tower

No way to count from here the number of guests
since I was the latest one
to watch the desert horizon sprout
a prick of glass which, as I neared it, swelled, soared
from the quivering mirage,
glistened as though a waterspout froze
while the sea around it parched into white sand.

The whole high-rise was veined with the arabesques
a streamlet's limber sinews
flex; throughout it ran webs of cirrus,
and under these, blurred as through a shower door,
the blush of every skin tone
warming the length of the cylinder—
the occupants I'd meet each day. Some at night.

The tip of the tower stemmed the sky's one cloud.
The twin folds of an ogee,
curving like parted curtains, girdled
the portal out from which blew a whiff of soaked
minerals, hinted with grass
and salt. Whose gleeful profligacy
unloosened such humid gusts where no rain falls?

—A question no sooner posed than swept away
or up the hollow column
wide as an ice rink and much too tall
for the top to be seen through a dense white haze.
Around this inner surface
spiraled a staircase covered and braced
by arching colonettes, hewn from the same rock,

and lined with the entryways to sun-flushed rooms.
Queued by the new arrival,
everyone stepped out onto the stairs,
physiques but loosely wound in rumpled chiffon.
In unison they mounted
the tower until they reached the next
room, leaving the first one vacant. That was mine.

Spartan furnishings: basin, desk, twin-sized slab,
all chiseled from the crystal,
cold and smooth on a skin no longer
naive to its nakedness. Hence a swathe of sheer
afloat in the air to clothe
my now-complicit tissues, anxious
both to tempt and to famish the shameless gaze.

Across the ceiling padded the soft brown soles
of another tenant's feet,
and a ripened olive suntan bloomed
through the wall. Land of the free, home of the nude!
Now any room was a lamp
and the body its lit wick, each breath
fanning its blaze, from each tongue a lick of wit,

waiting for when the sun, framed in a porthole
of unrestrained transparence,
sank at last in the earth. The heavenly
chambers flushed with peach and rose, diminishing
to violet, then to darkness
until the moonrise. Their facets shone
as if rinsed with milk. Indeed the sound of rain

led out to the stairs made dangerously slick
with what a taste, fingertip
wetted and raised to the shriveled lip,
proved to be water. It trickled down the steps,
fell from the vanishing point
above, lured us toward our neighbors,
shadows made substance, anonymous figures

meeting to give and take an essence of self
too subtle for barriers
save those both pervious and rigid,
revealing and concealing, blown through shifting
pressures, a candle flame's
elusive cypress, each limb seared raw
and fluid till limitations, and the dawn, broke.

At noon a new member comes, and clockwise we
corkscrew up the inverted
well, each room upstairs identical
except for the way the sun strays to the right
of the window, vanishes,
then reappears on the left, a full
circle, new height, and fresh tenderness at night—

the hours blear into the constant hum of quartz
bent to the point of yielding
a charge. The higher the cell, the more
the current prickles. We have never felt so keen,
receptive to the shiver
around us. I won't pretend to know,
having spent my heartbeats in private quarters,

more wisdom than that which surges from a tense
            piezoelectric thrum
      between desires—one for lattices,
one for rivulets. All the more poignant, then,
            how our incarnation grows
      clear, drained of its tincture. We are
but silhouettes of frost on glass, soon to melt,

though some believe we meld into the tower.
            Why does it end in a cloud?
      Where did I think the spiral would go?
Fires point themselves toward their own vanishing.
            I am saddened by the end
      of my revels, as we know them, yet
glad to join the structure in which they persist.

Night Fog

Within a summer afternoon
between the ocean and the sky,
radiant mountains of cumulus—
pearls in a heap a mile high—

construe from premises of air
a slope as mutable and sheer
as the no-less-visionary summit
lifted above the troposphere;

by night they crumble into fog,
lose altitude and pressure, blow
across the beach, the esplanade,
a surfer's clapboard bungalow;

they overrun a windmill palm
and every overhanging lamp,
dilute each bulb to an aureole,
unravel low enough to damp

the silhouetted walker's wind-
ward cheek, each inhalation cool
and sharp with salt. How redolent,
like syllables from Roman rule.

Ripples: Lake Merritt

Wishbone fluidities and clamshell furrows
merge while they roam the cityside lagoon,
rehearse how cosmic microwaves commune
eons before and after wars and pharaohs.

Streetlights that glance off the epilimnion
vibrato scrawl their glittering seismograms
a rower, arrowing through water, grooms,
degaussing the phosphor-soft aluminum,

then he withdraws, along with every walk
beside these ripples, headlights, moonrises,
last evening's minnows, roller skaters, roses
dyed blue, a gondola, its languorous wake.

Afloat on perpetual motion, say reflection
opens a quivering stage where actors meet
once more, where every dialogue falls mute
in a held gaze, where time is no affliction—

would it be better to share this movie-scene
perfection, spinning in a rumba, and never
the kind that mellows when the film is over
and twilight recollects the stars? How soon

the water's residual blue relents to mauve.
A heron, hunting, halts at the moiré weave.
Poised is the beak or pen each minor wave
excites. Both the neck and the wrist move.

Previous Winners of the New Criterion Poetry Prize

Peter Vertacnik, *The Nature of Things Fragile*
Brian Brodeur, *Some Problems with Autobiography*
Nicholas Pierce, *In Transit*
Bruce Bond, *Behemoth*
Ned Balbo, *The Cylburn Touch-Me-Nots*
Nicholas Friedman, *Petty Theft*
Moira Egan, *Synæsthesium*
John Foy, *Night Vision*
Michael Spence, *Umbilical*
John Poch, *Fix Quiet*
Dick Allen, *This Shadowy Place*
George Green, *Lord Byron's Foot*
D. H. Tracy, *Janet's Cottage*
Ashley Anna McHugh, *Into These Knots*
William Virgil Davis, *Landscape and Journey*
Daniel Brown, *Taking the Occasion*
J. Allyn Rosser, *Foiled Again*
Bill Coyle, *The God of This World to His Prophet*
Geoffrey Brock, *Weighing Light*
Deborah Warren, *Zero Meridian*
Charles Tomlinson, *Skywriting and Other Poems*
Adam Kirsch, *The Thousand Wells*
Donald Petersen, *Early and Late: Selected Poems*